UNDETECTABLE

✺

BRENT ARMENDINGER

UNDETECTABLE

✺

BRENT ARMENDINGER

NEW MICHIGAN PRESS
TUCSON, ARIZONA

NEW MICHIGAN PRESS
DEPT OF ENGLISH, P. O. BOX 210067
UNIVERSITY OF ARIZONA
TUCSON, AZ 85721-0067

<http://newmichiganpress.com/nmp>

Orders and queries to nmp@thediagram.com.

Copyright © 2009 by Brent Armendinger.
All rights reserved.

ISBN 978-1-934832-20-2. FIRST PRINTING.

Printed in the United States of America.

Design by Ander Monson.

Cover art courtesy Daniel Paige.

CONTENTS

Toxic Assets   1
Xeriscaping   3
The Year of the Dragon   6
Diagnosis   11
The Waiting Room   13
Homonym   17
Wrong Questions, *An Apology*   20
It Window   27
I Love You Remus Get Up   31
We Should Be Thawing out of Mountains   35
When the War Fails It Prays   37
Instant Messenger   46

Acknowledgments   51

TOXIC ASSETS

An acronym is a memory, the color
of someone else's blood—a fact
fell out of us and through
a hole in me. Neither virus
nor my death nor my survival
belong to me.

My body is sewn with red thread,
an acronym is someone else who
came before me, someone else
who acted for me—my debt
is coiled around a spool.

ACT UP: the breath between
the verb and the direction—
the disappearance
on which all urgency—that rage
that saved my life, I admit it,
I envy it, that bell
that clangs for me but not
inside me.

The letters slid together
and one poison made it possible
to live inside another—to adapt.
Our acronyms slid

into each other, our clapboard
house to guard elixir—
to fix the budget crisis
the governor proposes an estate sale:
he'd sell the ill for fuel.

Our bodies are in danger
the moment I know
that I somehow survived.

XERISCAPING

The quietness after fucking
filled the room with moths. A moth
is when we stopped breathing
long enough to be alive.
What if x equals
all the winged zeroes

we forgot
on the way to how old we are
divided by a drought? A thousand exhalations
to spend the way we choose.
What if we could?
A thousand breaths a day. The remainder
as what's human. A moth

wakes up inside a piano
like hearing without a mouth.
Wild was the wind, a radio
uninterrupted by air. Out there
is unwritten. A noise. Inside is
embarrassed and very late,
like a hospital. All those zeroes
falling down from the sky when I.

A moth goes back to sleep.

The problem with breath is breath is not
a metaphor. The poet
could live an hour or so outside
his iron lung, maybe twice
a week or only once a month.
The problem with an hour, the problem
with a zero. Above our heads

we hold our metaphors, umbrellas
fading in the sun, trying to steer it,
it's practically desert,
the slow, forgetful sky.

I came to you by walking
south, mailing my blood back north,
knowing it would dry
on my return address
before it stain your hand.
A stain, my zero. Not the color
you live in but a bridge
of wings to walk across.
Or a minefield.

Behind a window, what is a friend
outside the window, a bridge
inside an envelope. Oh friend,
what is a wing, a flat star
to press against your face—

careful not to bury it,
careful in the thaw.

Sometimes it's only memory
that listens hard, the wing
or train fall down. Sometimes
it's only winter to not relent
a leaf. This bruise
is who's inside it. You put me
on your shelf. A hospital
for moths. Carefulness
in the bruise, involuntary thaw.

Under the freeway
you can sell your breath
for a bucket of water
then pour the water in the river
we turned upside down. The we that wasn't
born here. A hand-me-down,
a parable.

THE YEAR OF THE DRAGON

I unlock the file cabinets. Type blue letters into gray boxes. I keep failing at starting from zero.° Gender, ethnicity, age, income, sexual orientation. My breath weighs on the keys, kneads inaudible questions into the hard drive.

° Arrow came first, that
before the noise we gave it.
The people in the waiting room
look around and wonder
where did Lady Day go?
How did the song get scratched
and who gave it to you,
that record?

Dear city, my zero
cuts away the shadow
from sidewalk, cineplex,
pedestrian, crane. But before
I hear my number I'm with Frank,
poor Frank, as gay in death as me
in life so why should I
skip lunch. He pulls me
away from that runaway
dune buggy and off we go I'm sorry
before "everyone and I
stopped breathing."

I empty my memory in the mailbox and buy a watch for the blank. On the dial, a whale swallows a puppet who wants to be a boy.

Starting at zero fails at keeping. The lights in their tubes hum too quietly. *Take this envelope and give us a call when you're ready to come and talk about it.* I sink into the calendar on the wall like it's made of sand. °°

°° Little vessels it gets so crowded
before you even swallow air.
A muffled song is crawling
through my arteries. Childhood
keeps wrestling with mud
underground. It climbs
through alveoli.

How do trees grow here?

The traffic light spills yellow into the sky. A woman on her bicycle stares, the question in her eye spreads into streetcar wire and tire scream. The sky absorbs every color but one. Antibody.°°° This is being pink under water, the blue bottom painted with black lines. Chlorine-stung eyes look up to the surface and the knives of the city go dull. A word is heavy in my blood. I remember the nurse.

°°° What do other alphabets
admit about causation?
Somewhere over the Plains States
the airmail gets wrinkled
by the rubber bands. How the letter E
buckles into an arrow
when it's read from right
to left, a feather
falling through the trachea
to the foot of a shut door.

Don't lift anything heavy for the next couple of hours. I thank her for drawing my blood, like I belong to her.°°°° I shoulder my bike up the stairs—my first boyfriend called it portage, like lifting a canoe out of a pond.

Some learn to deserve the tremor on their tongues.

°°°° Marrow shiver through
my perforations. Someone
take erasing paper to the news
before it wilts into documentary
or triathlon. My hair falls
on the sidewalk in a trail
of red ribbons, like the future
is one big Sagrada Familia
twenty blocks ahead of my shoes.
Frank continues on to the corner store,
while a poem tries to catch
the breath that's meant
for epidemiology.

I say what the paper said. I fall to the carpet. Holly puts her hand on my back and holds water to my lips. Daniel puts his fingers in my palm. My body is a silver parachute lifted by children in recess.°°°°° Tissue, telephone, take-out, sleeping pill. Their fingers keep me hovering low above the gravel.

°°°°° It gave us noise
before that, first came arrow.
Or when the needle skips
there's a door swung open through
Billie's impossible blues.
Passing thunder plays the left side
of her piano. Mortality
requires as much living
as dying, so put your whole hand
inside my brick. Quick
while we're eroding. Hawks know.
They circle our gray apartment
like love.

DIAGNOSIS

What a hidden memory is electricity,
lonely as an unflipped switch,
fetal as hope inside a camera.
In a dream a doctor scrawls
the syndrome erasing vowels
from our ventricles.
We pull the staple
from his tally like a splinter,
scrambling the ink
into tanks of oxygen.

Waking breaks the bulb
over our head with wet eyes
and underwear. Scan our face
for blood and filament,
our impossible birth
precedes us.
How did we get here?
Medicine swerving the molecules
in our body like a one clock.
We ferment inside a hush
that's louder than disco.

Oh Hester, they cut letters
out of our dresses now
before they sew the final A—

they pin the missing shape to our skins
until our skins remember
who's missing. Grafting
teaches an orchard to pretend—
heavy fruit only
makes it seem
to bend.

THE WAITING ROOM

> *first there was brightness,*
> *then it suffered;*
> *suffering invented shape.*
> —Brenda Hillman, "Sorrow of Matter"

each body is intended to fail.

We sit holding our pink tickets to unlock the fault
inside the blood.

I watch my blood spill into 3 tubes
every 3 months and wait for my body's translation
into measure of white cell and virus.

The plastic vials wait on a turquoise shelf
shrink-wrapped in lonelier plastic. Polymer
is a ghost of prehistoric ghost
torn from a nest of rock
near the center of the planet. Longing
to hold again a light that cannot be
touched. Fossils hush

the howl in the blood
in locked refrigerated rooms.

When I cut my tongue on an envelope
the telephone nurse advises
no kissing for 24 hours. Only plastic
and number can safely hold it,
the second at the cliff before the universe
in my blood. Counting is grieving

for light severed into shards of matter.

Early language was tied
out of rope. The first knots were not
words but quantities: population,
harvest, sunlight, land.

> bodies still the velocity of light inside of skin long
> enough to measure its approximate glow.

I mistake body for light, I name it
firm handshake and taut
belly and beg it to spill into me.
As a child I believed I could trap
light inside of me. Sour
and stiff after weeks under the bed,
the way a darkroom is putrid
rescuing memory.

I was afraid to spill and now
it's not permitted. The place you came from
before you had a name.
I can't let you taste it.

A virus intends
to make my body collapse
before I leave it. Others die
climbing out their widening pores.
Will I suffocate inside my skin?
Will hollow cheeks pour out
the stale light inside?

Each body is intended to fail.
To reach this moment of bending over
a star-pollinated canyon while it
blooms inside the lungs. The point
right before they burst. The purpose
between beginning and begun, ending

and ended. The body
marries its shadow
then evaporates.

HOMONYM

In the beginning was there begging?
The impulse to turn sound into bird.

Pigeons together
make gray silver.
Birds without flock cry out
the names of the lost: "–ody, w-
–ody—ody, w- w-."
A double-*you* fading into sky
and not the feathered string geometry
opening a cloud.

An exile from his body
until the sadness on his tongue
grew spikes.

"What if he fell down this staircase in me
but we called it flying?" Gull's feathers
were already clean before Swallow
licked them, the color of platelets in orbit.
A stray bird scavenged to find sugar
for another like him, but
berries turn to burrs—Out of the black

hole between Swallow and the emergency
room, a gradual emission of geese.

They honked the numbers of roads,
the flavor of potato chips, the time
of telephone calls, the kid thrill of a helicopter
landing. They gathered like Thanksgiving
dinner, physical—not eloquent.

Swallow knew if he took off his coat
he would turn into the floor. He longed
for a waking clock to ring through
the automatic door, a sunken moon
peeling through familiar blinds.

Not even that wish, the dark one,
of a flock around his bed,

singing, "No, No,
Why? Why?" when he could
finally be empty
of his difference from them.

It's hard to imagine words
like *again*. Gull emerged
with feathers hid under parka,
glasses, prescriptions. Swallow
offered to drive him to the pharmacy.

When Gull left the café
his napkin kept trying to fly

up, so Swallow weighed it down
with packets of jam. But the curtains
sea-frothed and the lamp outside
cut the temperature so fear
could take a breath. A few leaves
wilted in the shape of birds. Gull
stared into a wall, making a nest
there in brick where he could imagine
dreaming safely. One can be standing
a foot away from a deep well
and nearly forget the feeling of mud
against the forehead—not the fact.

WRONG QUESTIONS, *AN APOLOGY*

No, I don't want you to lie. In the sex
club they step through my body like it's gone,

                        the snow filling up a small hole called
                                more than today.

None of these boys is
standing on the sticky floor.
He's easy sideburns, he's a straw
and a quick nod of the head.
I'm dissolving in mineral
time. It stings them into primordial
crawlers. The coat-check guy
knows it, Nick Drake is singing
till quiet tunnels break
under the speakers
at five in the morning.

                        Nothing gets wasted after it leaves us.

The traffic lights pulse against the swollen night
because they always do. It's you
who's slower.

                        You have been off my radar
                            screen for a long time.

*

> I was born with it—
> you were, too. But it found me.

Last night

> what I liked

getting on a bus and a letter
I cut my tongue opening.

> It is radiant what the breath leaves behind.

It is fish and it is my father's
voice heard perfectly under
water. It is telephone on fire.

> Envelope, what pretended to be you
> ?

Steal my name and stick wishes
under their tongues. You want them to break
sound like opening prisons. Before
construction sites are clean, before the continent
shrinks and waves are dry brown leaves.

*

The body becomes a fact that it is not.
What is wanting to know why for?

> In summer what the temperature
> cannot hold. But this means
> *have, you, me* all change. Something
> passed through but not the lover. A tiny glass
> shattered or ear, *my numbers have been really good.*

A ladder is cellular, double-helix. Ending
when the child spoke its first word.
Two paper cups around a black
hole. Sitting on a stranger's stoop
makes me less.

> Your sweater matched the color of my eyes.

A sweat inside us and not
on us. I wonder where
our parents are. It is not
our black hole, though I want
to say yes. Burn within three
feet, a rule we learned
about attraction   maybe
say no.

> *Aren't you worried?*

You who got it from doing, you
know. The color of the accident spent time,
a month, fell through me in the guts
of town. When glass is not
a window anymore.
A narration of sand.
A shadow or a symptom,
heat on my back.
Can you be scared
of what you already know?
The girl standing too close
to the end
of roof.

These small [   ] home.
Do you know who you got it from?

The neighbor said her father and her small brother,
they too—shifting blood
all the time.
Dad slid the bag under his bed
so he could show Mom.

Eyes the color of mud
and dandelion. When she
looked into them, her face inside,
her old backyard. Her father
before cancer.

                        A fact pushes out of a cell—
                        Cotton not cum made it spill,
                taking some membrane with it.
                    Only being afraid gets wet.

It wasn't me
        shoplifting

               because   turns   every   is   was

                      A month wishes into a cell—
              A house piled up outside. The wind
through the trailer walls was louder than forks.
               Our voices had candles in them.
                          Equal three
                    we slept umbilical
            around the washing machine
            before membrane was with it.
               We unwound the TV's red
          barbed wire and sewed reasons
         for a boy to touch my ugliest
                          insect wings.

It wasn't drugs,
a picture of someone else's muscles
in my thumb and neck.

>   I don't know the population of the world
>   I just remember it,
>   a man at the podium counting the people
>   who are supposed to be fed by now.
>   The year is already gone.
>   We all ran outside to see our mistakes
>   falling white and frozen
>   through a hole in the future.
>   Some of us caught them on our tongues.
>   No more someone whispers
>   a black hand over red writing.
>   *It got you.* The melted snow
>   was rising like fingers.
>   Who wanted these fingers?

I bite my cheek a lot these days.

> every faggot on the school bus knows the way things *are*
> is a fast-moving river he will either drown in or run across,
>   a street erased from every map.

What makes you say *No*
is the mirror-image of begin.
Every particle has an anti-particle. They were born
together—we were too. It's so much easier
to repair. You're sick. Our garbage
gets so tender. Tea with cayenne
and lemon. Where you came from is

it splits so they can exist. stretching itself

across the water

      Luckily they all tested negative.
       When he goes to kiss you,
  Too smart for More confident Turn away
I'd say you're a real One wish I'm sorry Before
    next time, okay? Don't give him
     what he A real success story.

Who do you know?

           I'm hungry,
    I'm not thinking about what happened.

IT WINDOW

Who become the parents of the trespassing
possum? If not the lilies behind the lock
then the gluttonous street, the tires.
Inevitable breath blows ink around
on the map. It leaks through
covered mouths into people
on the sidewalk. None come home
from the future without retreat.

A window hangs between two
wishes. Alone is a wish
to steer the world
in a spoon, Another
to bake loaves out of halves.
Fingers and cock forget
they grew up in different
towns. Pour two pitchers
and try to drink from one.
A window won't make light
but flood over faces,
also the dark.

The bed painted wings on glass
so wishes took turns being aviary
and binoculars. Asking permission
to smoke spilled sugar

on the fire escape. Four legs
on a bicycle shrunk the stop signs
into kids burying pop cans
in the snow. Another's eyes
bent into a pool behind his spine
where Alone is learning to swim.
His underwater face, red and blue
lights in the fog, always rushing
to the delivery room.
This hospital mineral
flows through Alone
and Another, rises into a scar
under their elbows
in the shape of a key.
If the ambulance slowed
could it become harbor lights?
Would that be burying time?

Alone thought, how difficult to compose in the presence of Another.

Dear Another On your birthday sitting in the doctor's office the only thing that can make me smile under the fluorescent lights and worry is your face is the thought of your shape winding toward me from a block away sliding through seconds with your hips like the pendulum of a clock whose secret is imprinted on my forehead. I should always be a block away not here filling up calendars with what-if and

what-then. You say too early to close this letter with love but
I want to open it XOXO Alone

What if only half the recording enters
an ear filled with musical notations?
What would it take for the window
to be the wish? Dust gathers on the glass—
Make it not hide. Multiply the shine
into microscopes, pile them on the tongue,
enough for every bud to taste
the difference in seeing.

Losing count of moments the window sees them flicker—
(How does a wish shine from inside without shining
   from the past?)
Brighter than sex or weather time blurs
between the panes. None come home
from the future. Another remembers
frostbite, pulls a blanket
from the basement. Calls it Spring.
Sew it in the sill, say
it's still the window. Alone
throws rain.

Between the fabric and the water
pitchers pouring songs
are bottomless, unclung
to the fists of wishes. Radios

weld memory and mass
to the edge of velocity. Scatter
and spin, intersecting
with no limbs. A particle
wobbles against the atmosphere's
neck, trails burn
to show it was.

I LOVE YOU REMUS GET UP

I could never be your wolf
but I could find you faster—
it rhymes but it's not master.
I couldn't carry you
anywhere with my teeth, you know
the way my gums are, you don't want my babies,
I'm no woodpecker either,
I want to be suckled by you.

Every picture frame
I've ever hammered to a wall
makes a smoke detector fall down,
and though you'll leave me
it's not because I'm supposed to
sew you a sweater
or an apology
while you're off buying a sandwich.

Now I see that color is another
form of eczema.
And anyway
the wolf died.
There was a farmer but he had a wife,
at least she taught me a thing or two.
Romulus wanted real towers
not the fake kind that perforate sadness

instead of sky, poor Remus
just wanted Romulus to want his want
not to take harm so goddamned literally.

You prepare for war, like love,
by moving to a new town
you know only by latitude
and longitude. You leave the door
unlocked and stay in a hotel
down the street. It puts holes
in your mouth and your white eyes.
Remus jumped the wall
so now there's two of us,
floating head and tripping femur—
all we want is our real mother.

You keep a recipe book of antidotes
for every syndicated calamity, so
let's break our hip bones into egg shells,
assemble them into our mother
and sail her back along the Tiber.
When we fall down on the couch
with all our clothes on, we breathe
like the anemone we stare at
in the aquarium at the bar,
whose sore old waving tentacles
could rest inside a green gut
finally whole: you'll say

I'm the yellow one
and we won't save each other.

My friends have premonitions.
I'm looking in your baby book
for your senior citizen discount.
Our dicks are an outdated joke to us
Why would we need to touch them?

When you were 9 you wore your shorts
up above your belly button,
so conscious
of every camera
like a squad car
hoping the policeman inside
would rescue you
from his burned red forearms.
Look at our bodies, Dave:

they are so many open doors.

I know which one to put my ear against,
I know your hands are full
a cigarette a fizzy pop
cocktail a paper towel hey
don't drop that
don't bother coming when I knock
I know which way to fail.

My friends have premonitions.
Why would we need to touch them?

WE SHOULD BE THAWING OUT OF MOUNTAINS

My ghost walks through the door
hung around the neck of a man
who doesn't hear it breathe. A clock
spreads a room into longing.
How many misunderstood moons
visit our archives? Lost ethnographers
with very dirty fingernails.
There is a reporter with a hairstyle,
it gets in front of my heart.

The sun happened before I burn
too close to different skin. Do I
diminish in color? Take a compass
from my pocket, draw a ray against the wrong
edge of the world. Being gay
tries to erase a square before it opens.
Two lines stop being parallel
when one bends around my arms
in little half-circles behind my back—
What keeps them from intersecting?

For a moment I'm a stranger to gravity
I don't owe it anything. Language
is the sun we cannot sleep upon,
so when a tent catches fire, your father
wets his hands with his face

at the corner of the bed. Where do syllables
take us? My father said it too—
we were painting the garage,
arguing over color: *You sure have a way
with words.* Certainty makes us citizens,
oh the border bruises. Words
care for permutations we haven't
the milk to feed. We might
have evolved differently, still
the webs between our fingers glow.

WHEN THE WAR FAILS IT PRAYS

I.

If musculature is mother
and daughter of movement then it is not
touch we long for but its potential
loss who any swollen who
the not gonna never intended
to love sighed *Oh well* into the receiver.
Though us and them were hemmed
were *never we more than casual* the casualties
spilled into my apartment
through the alarm
clock radio. Mine others
sighed the never song or bungalow
mine others absentee. All self
could do was ice was turn
off the news which can never be new
if it's intended to be loved, unplug the telephone
and listen to ashes fall on redial.

Who crosses the river without a microphone
as in what exactly is the shadow
cast by Homeland Security but ice
never would have made it home from the bar
otherwise. Sky was spreading
to glass. Us and hem ran inside

without a condom but ice
never would have made it. The clouds
hemmed our phone numbers
down on ballot stubs, the clouds
the clouds the clouds themselves.
Hem ourselves heaved minus mine.
Cleaved, Minus, Others, Hem Us,
mine the me not gonna.
The clouds the clouds the clouds.

And in the wings the antiretrovirus
called *Homoland Security* is aiming x-rays
at our limp wrists on the conveyor,
may I see your boarding pass, may I see
your virus, welcome to the splicing
is seeing the skin from inside the blood,
may I keep your virus
away from people who are people
without virus for the duration
of this flight may I keep your people
with virus away from people.

II.

How people assemble doors,
how people resemble and scrape

the ice from each other's language.
Ice is melting under an umbrella
to be loved as an Other who is always
disappearing in ink who is long and leaking
a hole through the alphabet.
"I have resisted my comrades and their parties"
for an unpredicted face in a crowd where a signature
is disappearing for a face who is not
opposite that already and always
disappearing. There is longing
for recognition and there is longing
for recognition in refuting
the longing. Syntax
can't solve it. The fossil of
a whip and a noose and a handcuff
is in the cotton is in the outfit
that can stencil anything but a capital S
into a "slaveholding document."
An imperative: Do Not:
wants to slit a door in the guilt that seeps
through genealogy.
Warning and condemnation are easy
batteries whose rays crawl through a flashlight
in the shape of a Y, changing all the ours
into yours. Electricity
wants to suck memory from moon
whose light broke over the great

great-grandparents who broke the great-great-
grandparents who were broken. Who
were broken. Broken,

who were they?
Stay there,
can we stay there.

When the subject is the one who is breaking
and the object is the one who is broken
or an object is not even existing,
then there is a deeper broken, broken
of a human being not only deflated
but never even breathed
into a word. Breaking of:
their names which are not my name
which had better not be your name
did that breaking. Breaking of
does anyone know the names
of the people who were broken
who do not begin the sentence and the names
of the people who were being broken who
rarely even end the sentence.
A person is and was
a slave who is and was enslaved
by a slaveholder. A person
is subtracted by a person who does not want to be
a slaveholder who makes an accusation.

An accusation which leaves
the only person in a sentence
the slaveholder. And this is where
it freezes the ice that so easily
blades and declares it prior
because the only rain that happens
falls in the bar where ice is not hooking up
or felt or married.
Ice is not getting felt.
The ice equals frozen, the not
getting felt. And so there is rain
without thaw. And rain
does not intend a narrow river but the I
rests so much broken rain
on the isthmus. On the Against.

   III.

How people resemble and scrape
each other, war in the wardrobe
of failed love. The poet
was dressed as a court stenographer,
refusing to leave the house for Halloween
or wash his syntax for a week.

The confession ice had to pull
off mine others tongue so the not gonna

could watch mine others skyscraper on TV
conveniently played by me scraping
me, then yawn about how tiresome it was
how very Presidential. The storm
stilled the green branches
into shrapnel, ligaments of trees
trafficked the highway until the radio called it
impossible by any breath but exhaust.
A before O except after No.
The dawn held up its white flags a howl
slowed to choral, "Come back
come back come back" a refrain freezes
missing faces permanent.

If a cluster of crows
can be called a murder,
how many soldiers march a parade
into war? How many brothers
who don't go to college but pine
for wider fields than the smell of gasoline
and corn and a full-time job.

IV.

Strangers undress in front of us,
but cell walls break into a single unheardstream.
A story, like a photograph, is violence

when the not gonna no longer pause
to breathe when the molecules of oxygen coil
into sickles. When the self looked
into the newspaper ice could have frozen
what is already undressed or called an ambulance.
Touch me with mine others camera,
but in the end us and hem are not
each other's spine. Trumpets
instead of axes weep for bodies
under rubble. It seemed wrong
to scan the PLU's, rehearsing
excuses about the rent, going about our business
snaps a frame around the electric hood
on the internet, between the spring water
and the AA batteries. Why can't ice
recognize my taxonomy?

The silver click the newsprint the gonetrees
folded in the rack which borrows its name
from antlers of a deer the rack
which borrows its plastic from the goneness
unmolten in the natural history
is harms is squareness that sews
not electricity nor prison
but a hood of stares that unwinds
the wound through the flickering
where all that us deleted is undulated
in a hum and a zero and one.

v.

The vapor between rainfall
connects the dry gray parentheses.
Pile the ancestor and the moment of shock
on the same past tense. Before the bomb
lay down in a basket before the basket
hid behind the jukebox a woman
stole a second to stare at her own
hair and not the scissors in her hand,
only a second before the milk
on not her child's tongue caught
fire. Us and hem
each other's knot. Cleaved,
Minus, Others, Hem Us, mine the me
not gonna. Windows
double blacken at the snap
of the guillotine, elsewhere
begins to storm. The clouds
the clouds the clouds.

Dear preemptive frost,
time is shaking
a curtain vigorously.
The lunar eclipse forgave
our ice into slow lightning.
Convincing the not gonna to follow
an imaginary line. Put mine others

ear to dirt and translate quicksand
into volcano. Ice knows
love is not preemptive.
When the war fails it prays
in our hand failure
is a prayer in reverse.

INSTANT MESSENGER

> In my dream my body was only one hand, so close to zero.
<honeylune> In your body my dream was only one hand.
<honeylune> Your gaze is doing this to us.
> Remember a snow fallen drunk.
<honeylune> Me too, but sober I measure fire by remaining
<honeylune> its opposite.
> If it slides through take a vessel for me?
<honeylune> I'd love to, but a little tired tonight.
> Alone is bluster.
> You always erase a little steeple where your head is growing.
<honeylune> Some animals prefer
<honeylune> our tiny sadness magazine
> Let me remember the movement of grass
> swallow your silver emergencies.
<honeylune> I'm blue shifting smoke, tempted.
> I'm blue shifting smoke, no that's just economy…
> without my petals scraping bone.
<honeylune> As am I.
> Then he puts his hands on your shoulders and he feels
> a sharp wind.
<honeylune> Yeah.
> A storm of orphaned wings.
<honeylune> Maybe, but not tonight.
> You've been walking backwards since August.
<honeylune> I have?
> Rope is instantly shadow.

\<honeylune\> Well, timing is everything.

\<honeylune\> I measure fire by remaining its opposite.

\> Why are you the only red passage if you're so tired?

\<honeylune\> We are not beautiful or cozy.

\> This transit of light through wire.

\<honeylune\> Rope is instantly shadow.

\<honeylune\> Why does it matter to you?

\> Our faces are red from blood or candy.

\<honeylune\> I hear sand.

\<honeylune\> Well, if it's to happen it will.

\> I forget I'm a sky full of knives, ambulance.

\> Might as well slip my shell.

\<honeylune\> Don't say that, I'm not an easy castle.

\> Harm.

\> No one else is.

\<honeylune\> I don't believe that.

\<honeylune\> You've never met a forest from underground.

\> I memorize.

\> It ends as skeletal as stars.

\<honeylune\> and ...

\<honeylune\> why?

\> I belong to the fog horn.

\<honeylune\> Well, is close to zero a pattern?

\> Rope is instantly shadow.

\<honeylune\> Is it based on scratching?

\<honeylune\> What's the sun's breath?

\<honeylune\> A swan is paging you.
> Hi.
> We are busy weakness.
> He's funny.
\<honeylune\> I see.
> The sun's breath, I don't know.
> I'm a thousand windows waiting for fingerprints.

ACKNOWLEDGMENTS

Many thanks to the editors of the following publications in which some of the poems in this collection first appeared: *Bird Dog:* "Homonym"; *Can We Have Our Ball Back?:* "Instant Messenger"; *The Concher:* "It Window" and "We Should Be Thawing out of Mountains"; and *Hayden's Ferry Review:* "I Love You Remus Get Up."

Fragments of "Diagnosis," "The Year of the Dragon," "Toxic Assets," "When the War Fails It Prays," and "Wrong Questions" appeared in my essay "(Un)Touchability: Disclosure and the Ethics of Loss," in the *Journal of Medical Humanities.*

These poems are indebted to the flippant genius of Frank O'Hara. Thanks to Carmen Giménez Smith for introducing me to Frank and suggesting that I look to him for direction. "The Year of the Dragon" includes a fragment from "The Day Lady Died," about the death of Billie Holliday; "I Love You Remus Get Up" is a riff on "Lana Turner has collapsed!"; and "When the War Fails It Prays" quotes his poem "Hatred": "I have resisted my comrades and their parties."

The poet with the iron lung in "Xeriscaping" is Mark O'Brien.

"The Waiting Room" includes an epigraph from Brenda Hillman's book, *Bright Existence* (Wesleyan University Press, 1993).

In "When the War Fails It Prays," the slogan "Homoland Security" refers to a public health campaign for men who have sex with men in San Francisco. The term "slaveholding document" appeared in a stencil against gay marriage on various sidewalks in San Francisco. The reference to the bomb in the basket comes from a scene in *The Battle of Algiers*, directed by Gillo Pontecorvo.

"The Year of the Dragon" is for HL and DP. "I Love You Remus Get Up" is for DL. "We Should Be Thawing out of Mountains" is for JA.

Special thanks to Daniel Paige for his artwork, friendship, and acupuncture.

Thanks to Ander Monson and all the folks at *DIAGRAM*, a magazine that is a true labor of love and quirkiness.

BRENT ARMENDINGER is the author of *Archipelago*, published by Noemi Press. Like his hero, Frank O'Hara, he has won a Hopwood Award for his poetry. He is the founder of the Poem-Booth Project; for more information, call 1-877-EAT-POEM from the nearest pay phone. He teaches creative writing at Pitzer College in Claremont, California, and regularly orbits San Francisco.

❋

NEW MICHIGAN PRESS, based in Tucson, Arizona, prints poetry and prose chapbooks, especially work that transcends traditional genre. Together with DIAGRAM, NMP sponsors a yearly chapbook competition.

DIAGRAM, a journal of text, art, and schematic, is published bimonthly at <http://thediagram.com>. Periodic print anthologies are available from the New Michigan Press.

❋

COLOPHON

Text is set in a digital version of Jenson, designed by Robert Slimbach in 1996, and based on the work of punchcutter, printer, and publisher Nicolas Jenson.

www.ingramcontent.com/pod-product-compliance
Lightning Source LLC
Chambersburg PA
CBHW031429040426
42444CB00006B/754

9781934832202